The Gingerbread Man

KB275314

This book belongs to _______________

WiSe kids

Writing Uppercase Letters

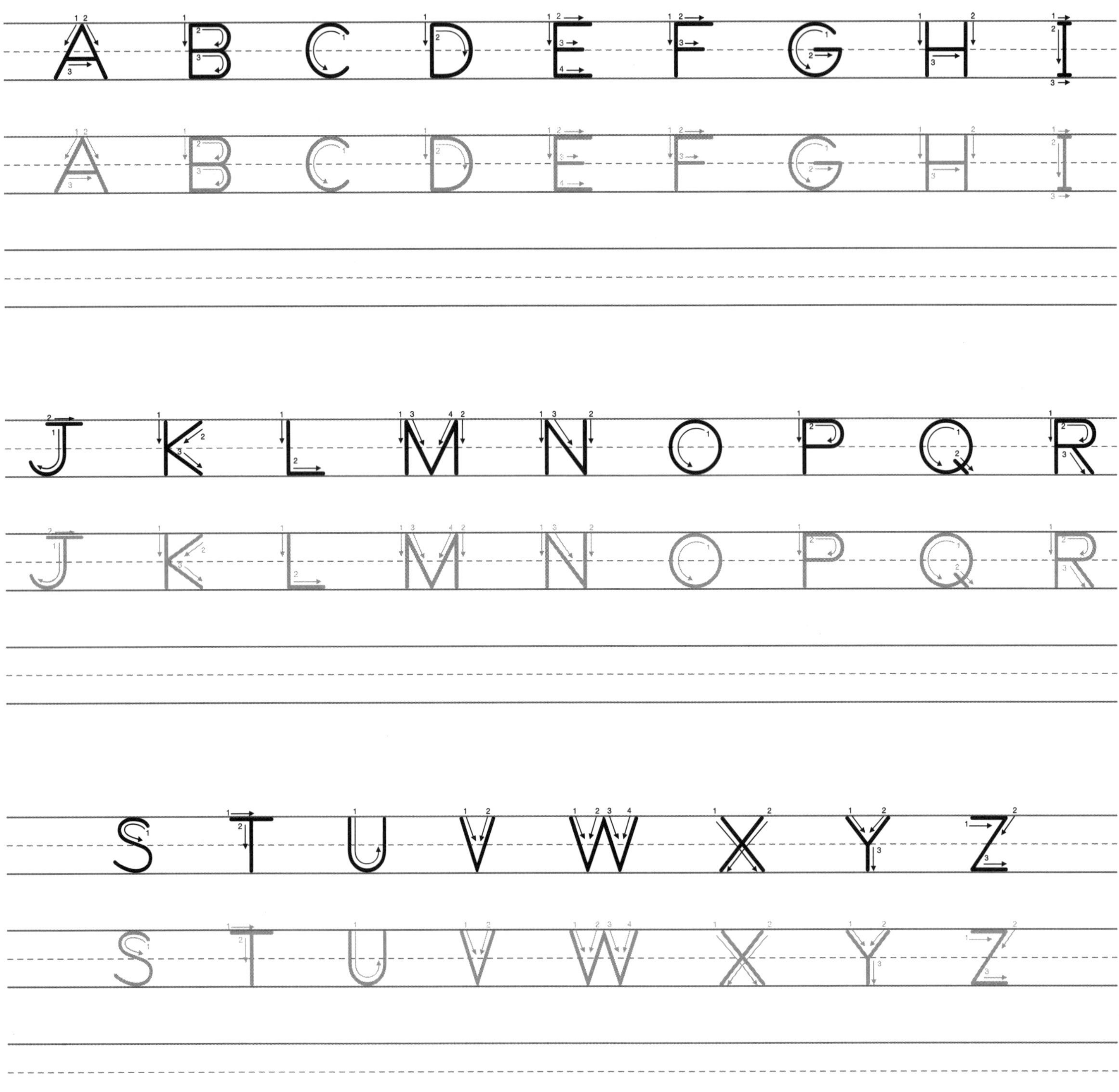

Writing Lowercase Letters

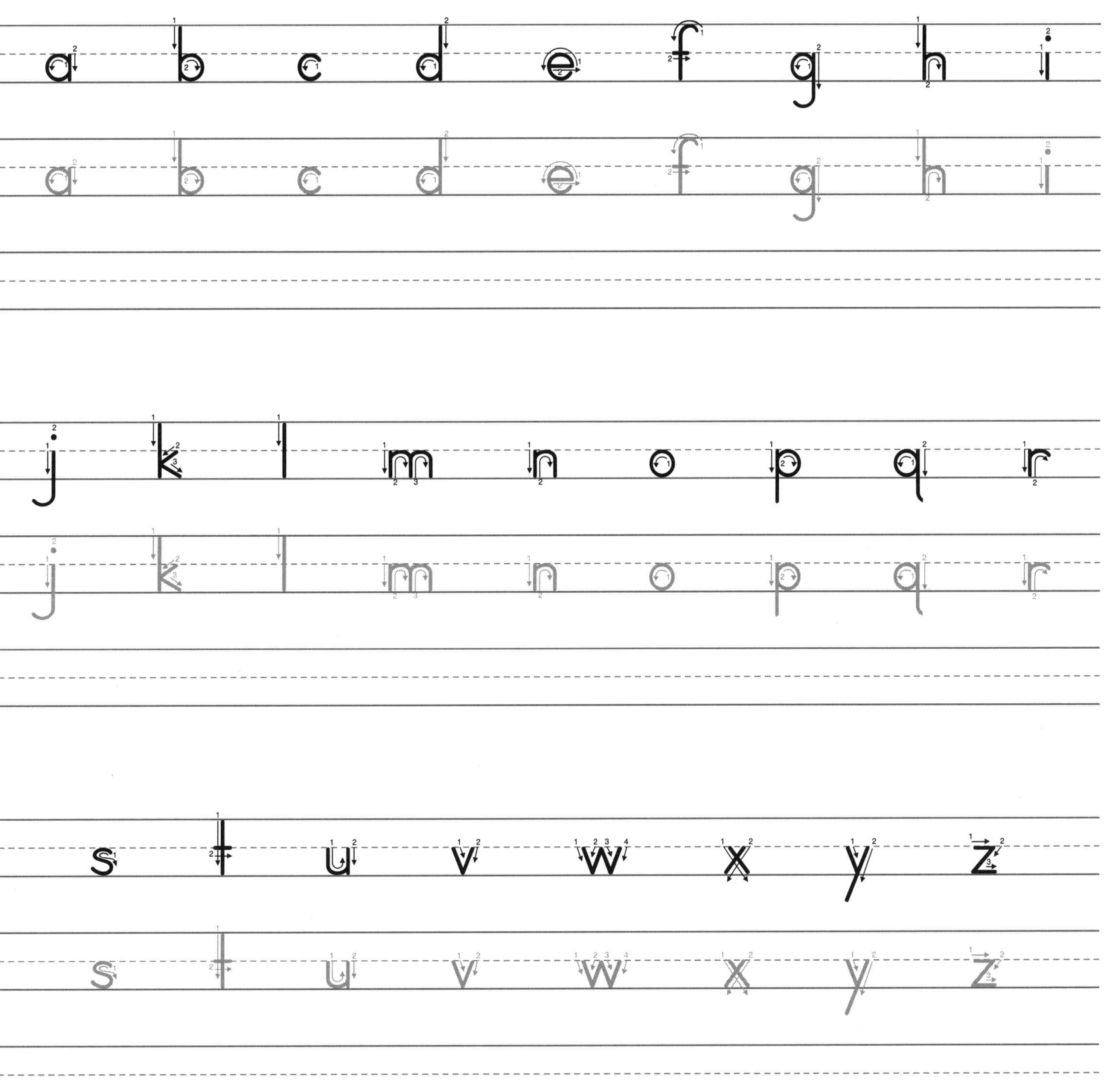

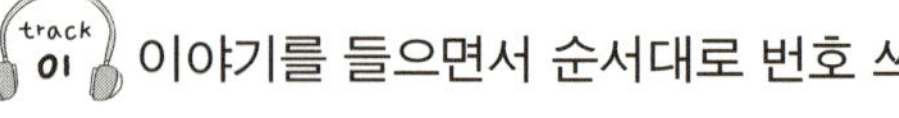

이야기를 들으면서 순서대로 번호 쓰기

1

 # What is a gingerbread man?

영어권 나라에서는 크리스마
스 때 사람 모양의 생강빵, 진
저브레드맨(gingerbread
man)쿠키를 가장 많이 먹는
답니다. 생강맛이 향긋하거나
서 겨울철에 따뜻한 차와 함
께 즐겨 먹는 간식이에요. 직
접 진저브레드 맨의 얼굴과
옷을 그리고 색칠해 보세요.

Activity 2 ## Decorate gingerbread friends!

직접 표정을 그리고 스티커를 이용하여 꾸며보세요.

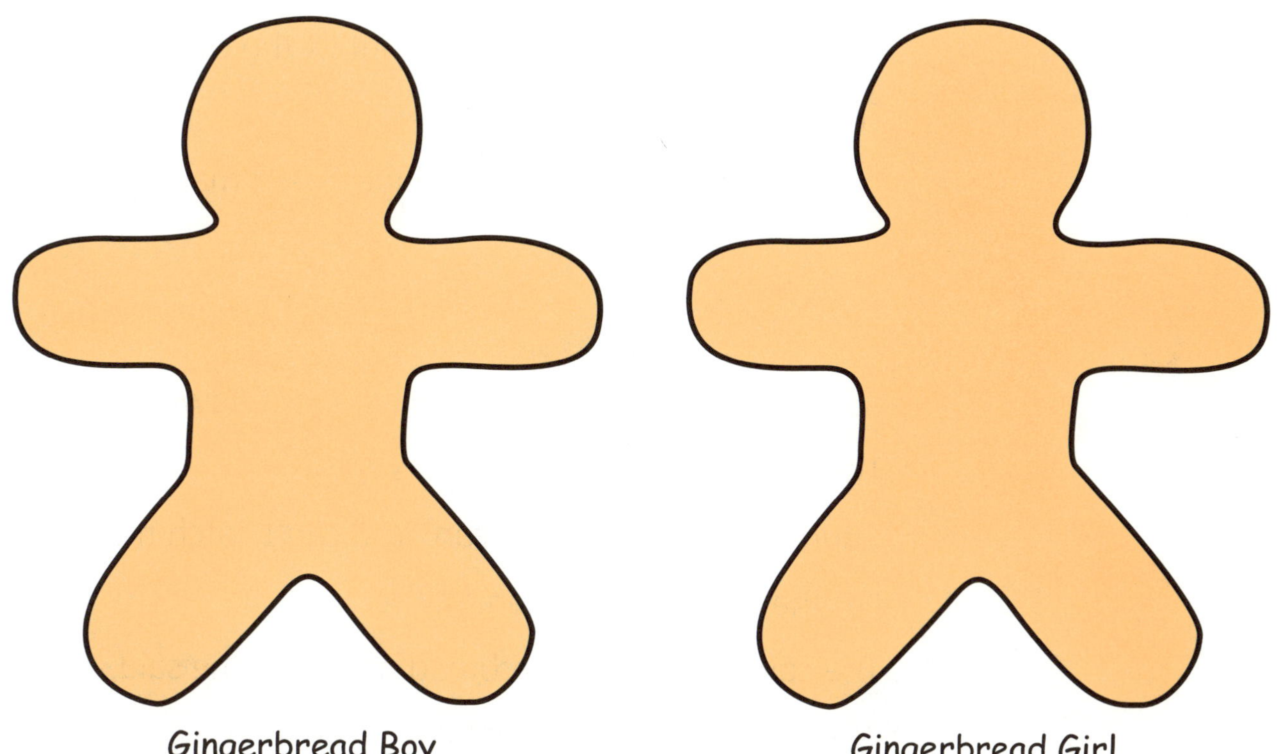

Gingerbread Boy

Gingerbread Girl

The Gingerbread Man

An old man and an old woman lived in a cottage.

The woman made a gingerbread man for Christmas.

"Raisins for eyes and cherries for buttons!

It looks great! It will be delicious," said the woman.

She put him in the oven.

"I can't wait to eat it. It smells so good," said the man.

Suddenly, the woman heard a little voice from the oven.

"Open the door! I want to get out right now."

"Is that you?" She opened the oven carefully.

The gingerbread man jumped out of the oven.

Then he ran out the window.

"Don't eat me!" yelled the gingerbread man.

"Stop! Come back!" They yelled and followed him.

The gingerbread man ran on, saying,

"Run, run as fast as you can. You can't catch me.

I'm the gingerbread man."

The cow saw the gingerbread man and she said,

"Stop there! I want to eat you, little man."

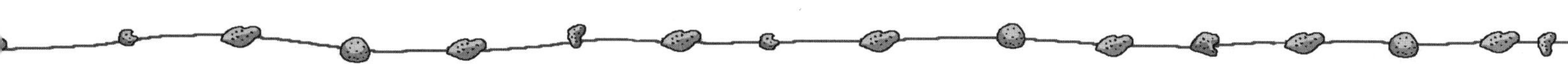

The gingerbread man ran faster and shouted,

"Run, run as fast as you can. You can't catch me.

I'm the gingerbread man."

Now the cow ran after him too, but he was too fast.

The pig saw the gingerbread man and ran after him.

"You make my mouth water. I want to eat you. Stop!"

The old couple, a cow, and a pig chased him.

The gingerbread man laughed and teased them.

"You can never catch me. I'm the fastest."

Then he reached a river and he got scared.

"Oh no! I will get wet. How can I cross the river?"

A fox came by and said, "I can help you cross the river."

"Sit on my tail," the fox grinned at him.

The fox began to swim and soon he got wet.

"Climb onto my back," said the fox and he did.

"You are too heavy. Jump on my nose," said the fox.

The fox tossed him up in the air and opened her mouth.

"Snap!" That was the end of the gingerbread man.

Let's Make Gingerbread Men!

진저브레드 맨을 만드는 데 필요한 재료들을 알아봅시다. CD를 듣고 따라 읽어 보세요.

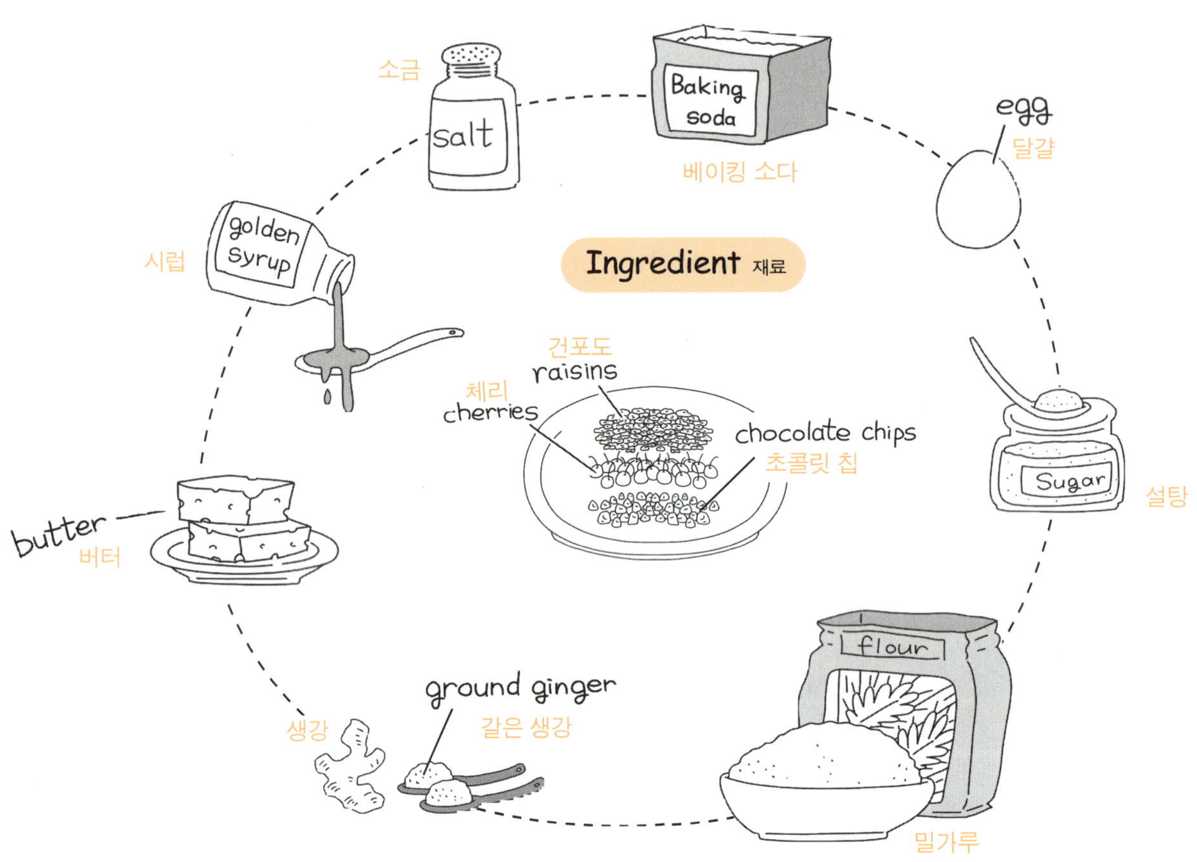

진저브레드 맨이 어떻게 만들어지는지 그림을 살펴 보면서 예쁘게 색칠해 보세요.

1 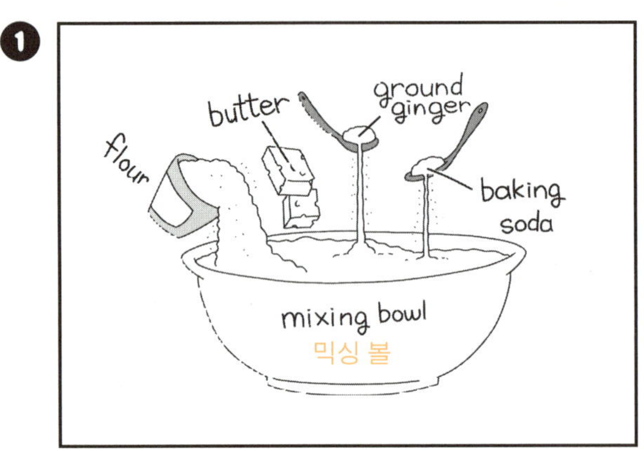

밀가루, 버터, 갈은 생강과 베이킹 소다를 넣으세요.

2 

재료들을 함께 잘~ 섞어주세요.

1st week

이번에는 설탕, 시럽, 달걀을 넣고 잘 섞으세요.

밀대를 가지고 반죽을 밀어보세요.

· 반죽을 진저브레드 맨 틀로 만들어 보세요.

건포도, 체리, 초콜릿 칩으로 꾸며 보세요.

약 10분간 오븐에서 구워주세요.

★    스티커를 찾아서 붙여 보세요. 나머지 그림은 예쁘게 색칠해 보세요.

The Gingerbread Man

1 An old man and an old woman lived / in a cottage. //
The woman made a gingerbread man / for Christmas. //
"Raisins for eyes / and cherries for buttons! //
It looks great! // It will be delicious," / said the woman. //
She put him / in the oven. //
"I can't wait to eat it. // It smells so good," / said the man. //

2 Suddenly, / the woman heard a little voice / from the oven. //
"Open the door! // I want to get out / right now." //
"Is that you? // She opened the oven / carefully. //
The gingerbread man jumped / out of the oven. //
Then / he ran out the window. //
"Don't eat me!" / yelled the gingerbread man. //

3 "Stop! // Come back!" // They yelled / and followed him. //
The gingerbread man ran on, / saying, /
"Run, / run as fast as you can. // You can't catch me. //
I'm the gingerbread man." //
The cow saw the gingerbread man / and she said, /
"Stop there! // I want to eat you, / little man." //

make(만들다)의 과거형

made　made　made

사람 모양의 생강 과자, 생강 빵

gingerbread man

raisin(건포도)의 복수형

rasins　rasins　rasins

cherry(체리)의 복수형

cherries　cherries

기다리다

wait　wait　wait　wait

smell(냄새/향기가 나다)의 3인칭 현재형

smells　smells　smells

hear(듣다)의 과거형

heard　heard　heard

목소리

voice　voice　voice

지금 당장

right now　right now

조심스럽게, 주의 깊게

carefully　carefully

yell(소리지르다)의 과거형

yelled　yelled　yelled

되돌아오다

come back　come back

see(보다)의 과거형

saw　saw　saw　saw

잡다

catch　catch　catch

1

An old man and an old woman lived /in a cottage. //
한 할아버지와 할머니가 살고 있었습니다 / 오두막집에. //

The woman made a gingerbread man /for Christmas. //
할머니가 진저브레드 맨을 만들었습니다 / 크리스마스를 위해서요. //

"Raisins for eyes /and cherries for buttons! //
"눈에는 건포도를 / 그리고 단추에는 체리를! //

It looks great! // It will be delicious," /said the woman. //
이거 근사해 보이는걸! // 맛있을 거야." / 할머니가 말했습니다. //

She put him /in the oven. //
할머니는 그를 넣었습니다 / 오븐 안으로요. //

"I can't wait to eat it. // It smells so good," /said the man. //
"나는 먹고 싶어서 기다릴 수가 없군. // 냄새가 정말 좋은걸." / 할아버지가 말했어요. //

2

Suddenly, /the woman heard a little voice /from the oven. //
그때 갑자기, / 할머니는 작은 목소리를 들었습니다 / 오븐에서 말입니다. //

"Open the door! // I want to get out /right now." //
"문을 열어줘요! // 밖으로 나가고 싶다고요 / 지금 당장." //

"Is that you?" // She opened the oven /carefully. //
"너인 게냐?" // 할머니는 오븐을 열었어요 / 조심스럽게. //

The gingerbread man jumped /out of the oven. //
진저브레드 맨이 뛰쳐나왔습니다 / 오븐 밖으로. //

Then /he ran out the window. //
그리고는 / 그는 창문 밖으로 뛰어나갔습니다. //

"Don't eat me!" /yelled the gingerbread man. //
"절 먹지 마세요!" / 진저브레드 맨이 외쳤습니다. //

"Stop! // Come back!" // They yelled / and fottowed him. //
"멈춰! //　　　돌아와!" //　　　　　　　노부부가 외치며 /　　　그를 따라갔습니다. //

The gingerbread man ran on, / saying, /
진저브레드 맨은 계속 달렸습니다 /　　　　　　말을 하면서요, /

"Run, / run as fast as you can. // You can't catch me. //
"달려봐요, /　최대한 빨리 달려보시라고요. //　　여러분은 날 절대로 못 잡을걸요. //

I'm the gingerbread man." //
내가 바로 진저브레드 맨이거든요." //

The cow saw the gingerbread man / and she said, /
젖소가 진저브레드 맨을 보았습니다 /　　　　그리고 그녀는 말했죠, /

"Stop there! // I want to eat you, / little man." //
"거기 서! //　　내가 너를 먹고 싶다고, / 꼬맹이야." //

Activity

What was it?

그림을 보고, 무엇인지 빈칸을 채워 보세요. 그리고 과거에는 어떤 모습이었는지
관련 있는 그림을 찾아 연결해 보세요.

1) 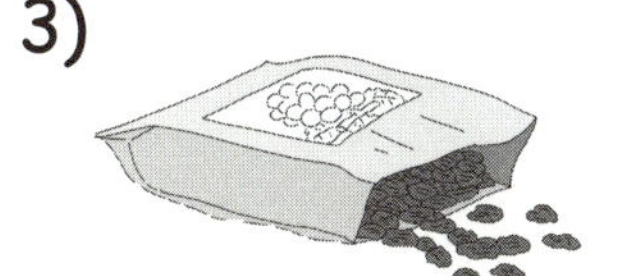

Now it is a ___________________.
What was it?

· ·

2)

Now it is a ___________________.
What was it?

· ·

3)

Now it is a ___________________.
What was it?

· ·

1

An old man and an old woman lived / in a cottage. //
한 할아버지와 할머니가 살고 있었습니다 /   오두막집에. //

The woman made a gingerbread man / for Christmas. //
할머니가 진저브레드 맨을 만들었습니다 /   크리스마스를 위해서요. //

"Raisins for eyes and cherries for buttons! //
"눈에는 건포도를 그리고 단추에는 체리를! //

It looks great! // It will be delicious," / said the woman. //
이거 근사한 걸! //   맛있을 거야." /   할머니가 말했습니다. //

She put him in the oven. //
할머니는 그를 오븐 안으로 넣었습니다. //

"I can't wait to eat it. // It smells so good," / said the man. //
"나는 먹고 싶어서 기다릴 수가 없군. //   냄새가 정말 좋은걸." /   할아버지가 말했어요. //

2

Suddenly, / the woman heard a little voice / from the oven. //
그때 갑자기, /   할머니는 작은 목소리를 들었습니다 /   오븐에서 말입니다. //

"Open the door! // I want to get out / right now." //
"문을 열어줘요! //   밖으로 나가고 싶다고요 /   지금 당장." //

"Is that you?" // She opened the oven / carefully. //
"너인 게냐?" //   할머니가 오븐을 열었습니다 /   조심스럽게. //

The gingerbread man jumped out of the oven. //
진저브레드 맨이 오븐 밖으로 뛰쳐나왔습니다. //

Then / he ran out the window. //
그리고는 /   그는 창문 밖으로 뛰어나갔습니다. //

"Don't eat me!" / yelled the gingerbread man. //
"절 먹지 마세요!" /   진저브레드 맨이 외쳤습니다. //

"Stop! // Come back!" // They yelled / and followed him. //

"멈춰! // 돌아와!" // 노부부가 외치며 / 그를 따라갔습니다. //

The gingerbread man ran on, / saying, /

진저브레드 맨은 계속 달렸습니다 / 말을 하면서요, /

"Run, / run as fast as you can. // You can't catch me. //

"달려봐요, / 최대한 빨리 달려보시라고요. // 여러분은 날 절대로 못 잡을걸요. //

I'm the gingerbread man." //

내가 바로 진저브레드 맨이거든요." //

The cow saw the gingerbread man / and she said, /

젖소가 진저브레드 맨을 보았습니다 / 그리고 그녀는 말했죠. /

"Stop there! // I want to eat you, / little man." //

"거기 서! // 내가 너를 먹고 싶다고, / 꼬맹이야." //

Activity

Find Opposites

다음 단어들의 반대말을 쓰고, 번호를 이용하여 gingerbread man이 하는 말을 완성해 보세요.

do	↔	_ _ _ _ 9
man	↔	_ _ _ _ 10 8
here	↔	_ _ _ _ 4 6 7
I	↔	_ _ _ 2
close	↔	_ _ _ _ 1 5 3

15

1

______ ______ man and ______ old woman ______ a cottage.

The woman ______ a gingerbread man ______.

"Raisins ______ and cherries ______!

It ______ great! It will be ______," said the woman.

She ______ him ______ the oven.

"I ______ ______ eat it. It ______ good," said the man.

2

Suddenly, the woman ______ a little ______ the oven.

"______ the door! I want to ______ right now."

"______ you?" She opened ______ carefully.

The gingerbread man ______ the oven.

______ he ______ the window.

"______ eat me!" ______ the ______ man.

"Stop! Come ________!" They yelled and ________ ________ .

The gingerbread man ________ ________ ,

"Run, run ________ fast ________ you ________ . You ________ catch me.

________ ________ gingerbread man."

The cow ________ the gingerbread man and she ________ ,

" ________ ________ ! I ________ to eat you, ________ man."

Activity
Spelling Errors

영어 철자(spelling)를 주의 깊게 보세요. 철자가 올바르게 쓰여 있는 공간만 예쁘게 색칠해 보세요.

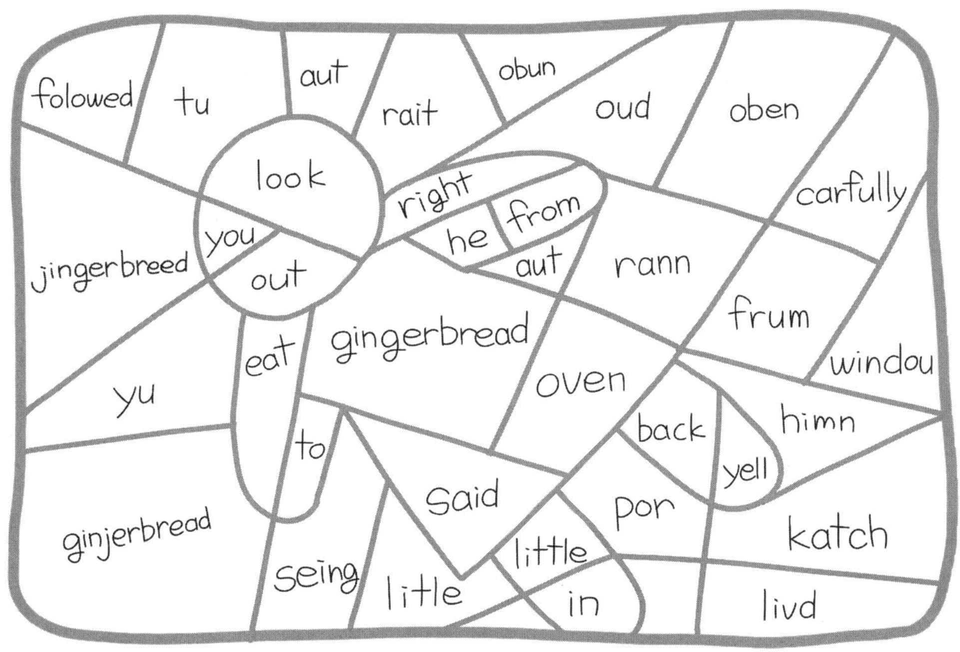

Q. What can you find from this picture?

A. I can find a ________ ________ .

1

한 할아버지와 할머니가 살고 있었습니다 / 오두막집에. //

할머니가 진저브레드 맨을 만들었습니다 / 크리스마스를 위해서요. //

"눈에는 건포도를 / 그리고 단추에는 체리를! //

이거 근사해 보이는걸! // 맛있을 거야." / 할머니가 말했습니다. //

할머니는 그를 오븐 안으로 넣었습니다. //

"먹고 싶어서 기다릴 수가 없군. // 냄새가 정말 좋은걸." / 할아버지가 말했어요. //

2

그때 갑자기, / 할머니는 작은 목소리를 들었습니다 / 오븐에서 말입니다. //

"문을 열어줘요! // 밖으로 나가고 싶다고요 / 지금 당장." //

"너인 게냐?" // 할머니가 오븐을 열었습니다 / 조심스럽게요. //

진저브레드 맨이 오븐 밖으로 뛰쳐나왔습니다. //

그리고는 / 그는 창문 밖으로 뛰어나갔습니다. //

"절 먹지 마세요!" / 진저브레드 맨이 외쳤습니다. //

3

"멈춰! // 돌아와!" // 노부부가 외치며 / 그를 따라갔습니다. //

진저브레드 맨은 계속 달렸습니다 / 말을 하면서요, /

"달려봐요, / 최대한 빨리 달려보시라고요. // 여러분은 날 절대로 못 잡을걸요. //

내가 바로 진저브레드 맨이거든요." //

젖소가 진저브레드 맨을 보았습니다 / 그리고 그녀는 말했죠. /

"거기 서! // 내가 너를 먹고 싶다고, / 꼬맹이야." //

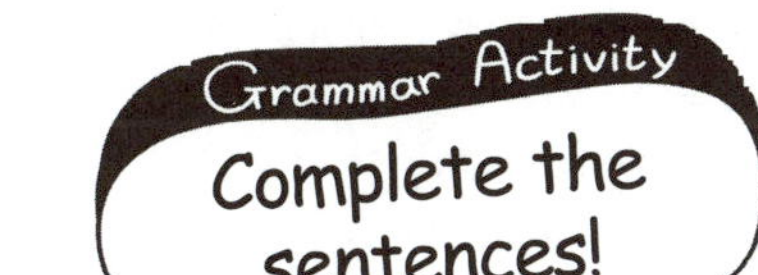

알맞은 단어를 골라 문장을 완성하세요.

1. An old man and old woman (liveed, lived, livd) in a cottage.

2. The woman (maked, makd, made) a gingerbread man for Christmas.

3. The old woman (put, putted, puted) him in the oven.

4. The gingerbread man (runned, runed, ran) out the window.

5. The old man (sayed, said, sayd) to the woman.

6. The cow (seed, saw, see) the gingerbread man.

7. The old couple (yelled, yellled, yellt) loudly.

8. Suddenly, the old woman (heared, heard, herd) a little voice.

Fill in the blanks. 빈 칸에 알맞은 단어를 고르세요.

1. The old woman made a _________________ for Christmas.

   a. chocolate cake   b. gingerbread man   c. Christmas tree   d. delicious cookie

2. The old woman used _________ for eyes and _____________ for buttons.

   a. chocolate, cherries   b. cherries, raisins

   c. raisins, cherries   d. raisins, candies

3. The gingerbread man could _________________.

   a. run and talk   b. sing and dance

   c. jump and sleep   d. make and yell

4. _____________ couldn't wait to eat the gingerbread man because it smelled so good.

   a. The gingerbread man   b. The cow   c. The woman   d. The man

5. _______________ yelled and followed _________________________.

   a. The gingerbread man, the old man   b. The old woman, the old man

   c. The old couple, the gingerbread man   d. The gingerbread man, the old couple

6. _____________________ wanted to eat the gingerbread man.

   a. The cow   b. The old man   c. The old woman   d. The old couple and the cow

7. The gingerbread man could run ____________.

   a. fast   b. slowly   c. loudly   d. carefully

True or False? 내용이 맞으면 T, 틀리면 F에 동그라미 하세요.

8. The old man ate the gingerbread man on Christmas day.　　T / F

9. The old couple was faster than the gingerbread man.　　T / F

Who did it? 다음 문장을 잘 읽고, 누가 한 말인지 이름을 써 보세요.

the old man　　the old woman　　the gingerbread man　　the cow

10.
It looks great!
It will be delicious.

____

11.
Run, run as fast as you can.
You can't catch me.

____

12.
I want to eat you,
little man.

____

Unscramble the sentences. 다음 단어들을 이용하여 문장을 완성해 보세요.

★ 문장이 다 끝난 뒤에는 마침표(.) 또는 느낌표(!)를 찍어 주세요.

13. woman, oven, The, voice, the, a, heard, little, from, .

____
- -
____

14. jumped, out, gingerbread, The, man, the, of, oven, .

____
- -
____

15. as, can, !, Run, fast, as, you

____
- -
____

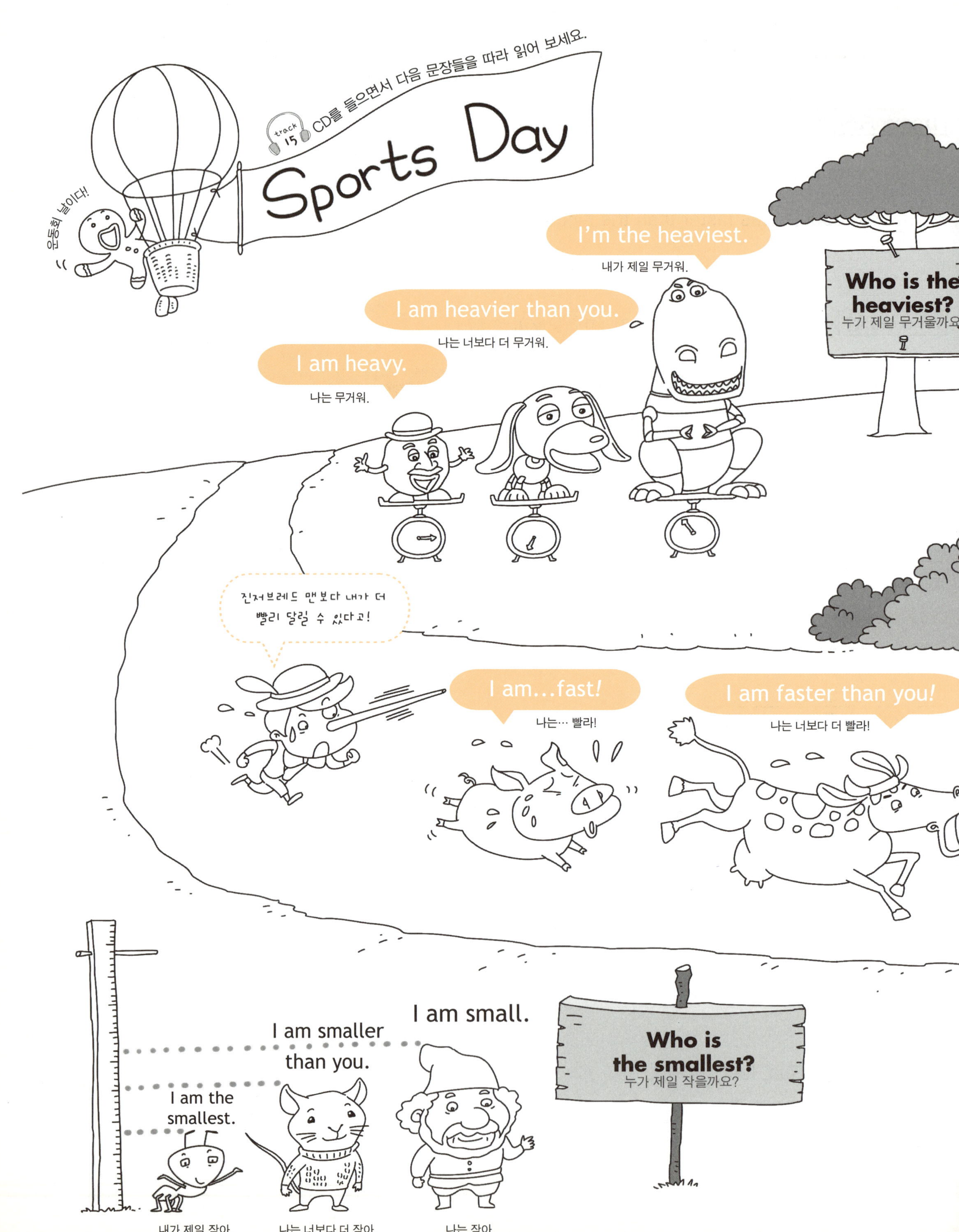
CD를 들으면서 다음 문장들을 따라 읽어 보세요.
track 15
Sports Day
얀듯히 날이다!
I'm the heaviest.
내가 제일 무거워.
I am heavier than you.
나는 너보다 더 무거워.
I am heavy.
나는 무거워.
Who is the heaviest?
누가 제일 무거울까요?
진저브레드 맨보다 내가 더 빨리 달릴 수 있다고!
I am...fast!
나는… 빨라!
I am faster than you!
나는 너보다 더 빨라!
I am small.
I am smaller than you.
I am the smallest.
Who is the smallest?
누가 제일 작을까요?
내가 제일 작아.
나는 너보다 더 작아.
나는 작아.

2nd week

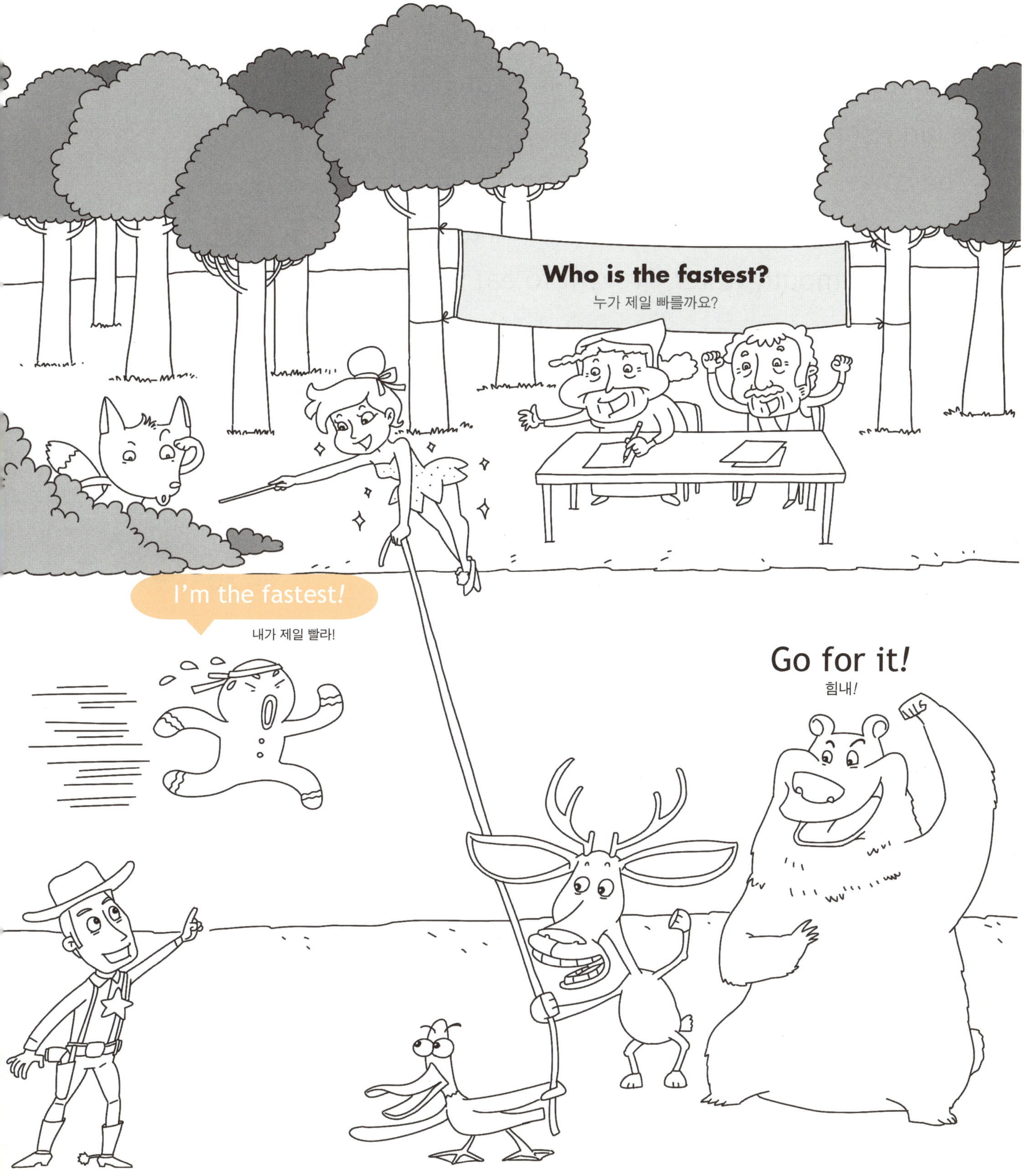

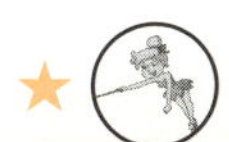

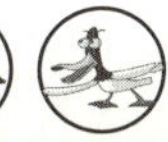

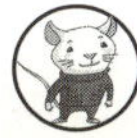

★ 스티커를 찾아서 붙여 보세요. 나머지 그림은 예쁘게 색칠해 보세요.

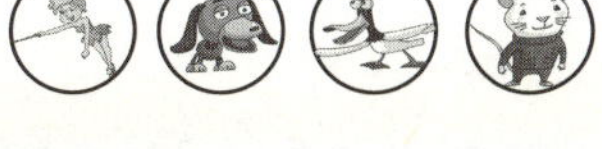

4 The gingerbread man ran faster / and shouted, /
"Run, / run as fast as you can. // You can't catch me. //
I'm the gingerbread man." //
Now / the cow ran after him too, / but he was too fast. //
The pig saw the gingerbread man / and ran after him. //
"You make my mouth water. // I want to eat you. // Stop!" //

5 The old couple, / a cow, / and a pig chased him. //
The gingerbread man laughed / and teased them. //
"You can never catch me. // I'm the fastest." //
Then / he reached a river / and he got scared. //
"Oh no! // I will get wet. // How can I cross the river?" //
A fox came by / and said, / "I can help you cross the river." //

6 "Sit on my tail," / the fox grinned at him. //
The fox began to swim / and soon he got wet. //
"Climb onto my back," / said the fox / and he did. //
"You are too heavy. // Jump on my nose," / said the fox. //
The fox tossed him up / in the air / and opened her mouth. //
"Snap!" // That was the end of the gingerbread man. //

fast 빠른 / **faster** 더 빠른 / **fastest** 가장 빠른

fast faster fastest

두 사람, 남녀 커플

couple couple couple

tease(놀리다)의 과거형

teased teased teased

무서운, 두려운

scared scared scared

~를 건너가다

cross cross cross

grin(소리 없이 씨익 웃다)의 과거형

grinned grinned

toss(~를 가볍게 던지다)의 과거형

tossed tossed tossed

~를 뒤쫓다 ＊**ran**은 **run**(뛰다)의 과거형

ran after ran after

chase(뒤쫓다)의 과거형

chased chased chased

reach(도착하다)의 과거형

reached reached

젖다

get wet get wet

꼬리

tait tait tait tait

오르다, 올라가다

climb ctimb climb

휙(잽싸게 움직여서 낚아채는 것)

snap snap snap

4

The gingerbread man ran faster/and shouted,/
진저브레드 맨이 더 빨리 달렸습니다 /   그리고 소리쳤어요. //

"Run,/run as fast as you can.// You can't catch me.//
"달려봐요, /   최대한 빨리 달려보시라고요. //   당신들은 날 잡지 못할걸요. //

I'm the gingerbread man."//
난 진저브레드 맨이거든요."//

Now/the cow ran after him too,/but he was too fast.//
이제 /   젖소도 그를 뒤쫓아갔습니다 /   하지만 그는 너무 빨랐습니다. //

The pig saw the gingerbread man/and ran after him.//
돼지가 진저브레드 맨을 보았습니다 /   그리고는 그를 쫓아갔습니다. //

"You make my mouth water.// I want to eat you.// Stop!"//
"넌 날 군침 돌게 만드는 구나. //   나는 널 먹고 싶어. //   멈춰!" //

5

The old couple,/a cow,/and a pig chased him.//
노부부, /   젖소, /   그리고 돼지가 그를 쫓아갔습니다. //

The gingerbread man laughed/and teased them.//
진저브레드 맨이 웃었어요 /   그리고 그들을 놀려댔습니다. //

"You can never catch me.// I'm the fastest."//
"너희들은 날 절대로 못 잡는다니까. //   내가 가장 빠르거든."//

Then/he reached a river/and he got scared.//
그때 /   그는 강가에 다다랐습니다 /   그러자 그는 무서워졌죠. //

"Oh no!// I will get wet.// How can I cross the river?"//
"아, 이런! //   내가 젖겠는걸. //   어떻게 이 강을 건너지?" //

A fox came by/and said,/"I can help you/cross the river."//
여우가 지나가다가 /   말했어요. /   "내가 널 도와줄 수 있어 /   강을 건너는 것을." //

6

"Sit on my tail," / the fox grinned at him. //

"내 꼬리 위에 앉아." /　　　　　여우가 그를 보면서 씨익 웃었습니다. //

The fox began to swim / and soon the he got wet. //

여우는 헤엄치기 시작했습니다 /　　　그러자 곧 그는 젖게 되었습니다. //

"Climb onto my back," / said the fox / and he did. //

"내 등 위로 올라오렴." /　　　여우가 말했습니다 /　　　그러자 그는(진저브레드 맨은) 그렇게 했습니다. //

"You are too heavy. // Jump on my nose," / said the fox. //

"넌 너무 무거워. //　　　　내 코 위로 뛰어올라와." /　　　여우가 말했습니다. //

The fox tossed him up / in the air / and opened her mouth. //

여우는 그를 위로 가볍게 던져올렸고 /　　　공중으로 /　　　그리고는 입을 벌렸습니다. //

"Snap!" // That was the end of the gingerbread man. //

"휙!" //　　　그게 바로 진저브레드 맨의 마지막이었습니다. //

Activity
Unscramble words

결국 영리한 여우가 혼자 진저브레드를 먹게 됐네요. 여우가 무슨 말을 했는지, 아래 뒤섞여 있는 낱말들을 순서대로 다시 써 보면 알 수 있답니다. 회색으로 표시된 글자만을 모아 순서대로 써 보세요.

1. oplcue　　□ □ [u] [l] ☐　(8, 3)
2. tmhou　　□ ▢ □ □ □　(7)
3. staf　　□ □ ▢ □　(9)
4. tis　　□ ▢ □　(4)
5. sedcar　　□ ▢ □ □ □ ▢　(5, 1)
6. rveir　　□ □ □ ▢ □　(2)
7. rai　　□ ▢ □　(6)

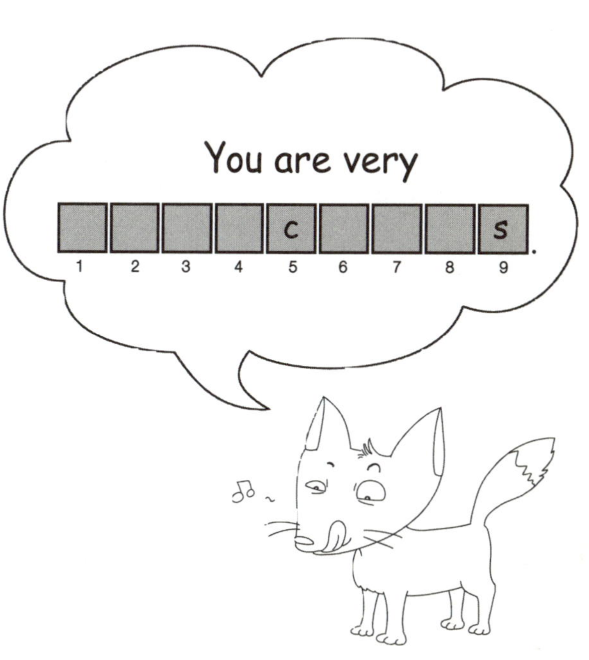

4

The gingerbread man ran faster / and shouted, /
진저브레드 맨이 더 빨리 달렸습니다 /　그리고 소리쳤어요. //

"Run, / run as fast as you can. // You can't catch me. //
"달려봐요, /　최대한 빨리 달려보시라고요. //　당신들은 날 잡지 못할걸요. //

I'm the gingerbread man." //
난 진저브레드 맨이거든요." //

Now / the cow ran after him too, / but he was too fast. //
이제 /　젖소도 그를 뒤쫓아갔습니다. /　하지만 그는 너무 빨랐습니다. //

The pig saw the gingerbread man / and ran after him. //
돼지가 진저브레드 맨을 보았습니다 /　그리고는 그를 쫓아갔습니다. //

"You make my mouth water. // I want to eat you. // Stop!" //
"넌 날 군침 돌게 만드는구나. //　나는 널 먹고 싶어. //　멈춰!" //

5

The old couple, a cow, and a pig chased him. //
노부부, 젖소, 그리고 돼지가 그를 쫓아갔습니다. //

The gingerbread man laughed / and teased them. //
진저브레드 맨이 웃었어요 /　그리고 그들을 놀려댔습니다. //

"You can never catch me. // I'm the fastest." //
"너희들은 날 절대로 못 잡는다니까. //　내가 가장 빠르거든." //

Then / he reached a river / and he got scared. //
그때 /　그는 강가에 다다랐습니다 /　그러자 그는 무서워졌죠. //

"Oh no! // I will get wet. // How can I cross the river?" //
"아, 이런! //　내가 젖겠는걸. //　어떻게 이 강을 건너지?" //

A fox came by and said, / "I can help you cross the river." //
여우가 지나가다가 말했어요. /　"네가 강을 건너는 것을 내가 도와줄 수 있어." //

6

"Sit on my tail," / the fox grinned at him. //

"내 꼬리 위에 앉아." /　　여우가 그를 보면서 씨익 웃었습니다. //

The fox began to swim / and soon he got wet. //

여우는 헤엄치기 시작했습니다 /　　그러자 곧 그는 젖게 되었습니다. //

"Climb onto my back," / said the fox / and he did. //

"내 등 위로 올라오렴." /　　여우가 말했습니다, /　　그러자 그는 그렇게 했습니다. //

"You are too heavy. // Jump on my nose," / said the fox. //

"넌 너무 무거워. //　　내 코 위로 뛰어올라와." /　　여우가 말했습니다. //

The fox tossed him up in the air / and opened her mouth. //

여우는 그를 공중 위로 가볍게 던져 올렸습니다 /　　그리고는 입을 벌렸습니다. //

"Snap!" // That was the end of the gingerbread man. //

"휙!" //　　그게 바로 진저브레드 맨의 마지막이었습니다. //

Activity
The letter from the gingerbread man

할머니가 정성스럽게 만든 진저브레드 맨이 도망가고 말았어요. 진저브레드 맨이 할머니에게 남긴 편지 한 통! 어떤 내용인지 순서에 맞춰 다시 써 보세요. 문장이 다 끝난 뒤에는 마침표나 느낌표를 꼭 찍어주세요.

Dear Grandma,

1. Christmas, for, made, You me, .
2. But, don't, eat, please, me, .
3. run, fast, can, very, I, .
4. me, never, You, catch, can, .
5. don't, me, Please, follow, !
6. Christmas, !, Merry

Sincerly,
Gingerbread Man

Dear Grandma,

1. You made
2.
3.
4.
5.
6.

Sincerly,
Gingerbread Man

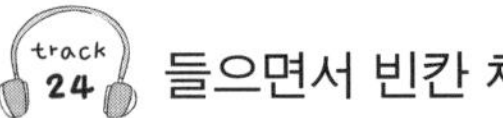

4 The __________ man ran ________ and ________,

"________, run ____ fast ____ you can. You ____ catch ____.

I'm ____ gingerbread ________."

________ the ____ ran ____ him ____, he ____ fast.

The ____ saw the gingerbread man ________ him.

"You ____ my ________. I want to eat you. ____!"

5 The old ________, a cow, and a pig ________.

The gingerbread man ________ and ________ them.

"You can ________ me. I'm the ________."

Then he ________ a river and he ________.

"Oh no! I ________ wet. How ____ I ____ the ________?"

A fox ________ and said, "I can ____ you cross the ________."

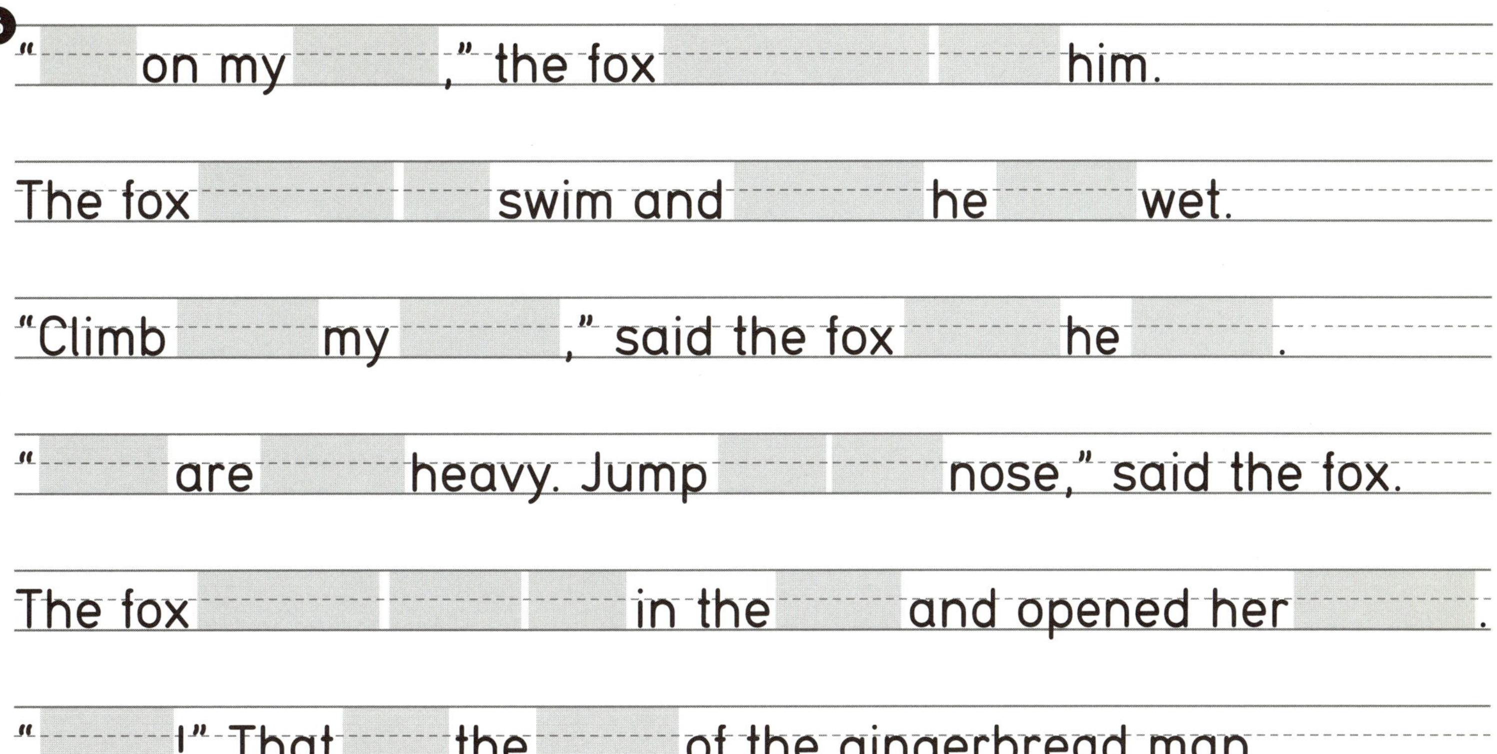

"_____ on my _____," the fox _____ him.

The fox _____ swim and _____ he _____ wet.

"Climb _____ my _____," said the fox _____ he _____ .

"_____ are _____ heavy. Jump _____ _____ nose," said the fox.

The fox _____ in the _____ and opened her _____ .

"_____ !" That _____ the _____ of the gingerbread man.

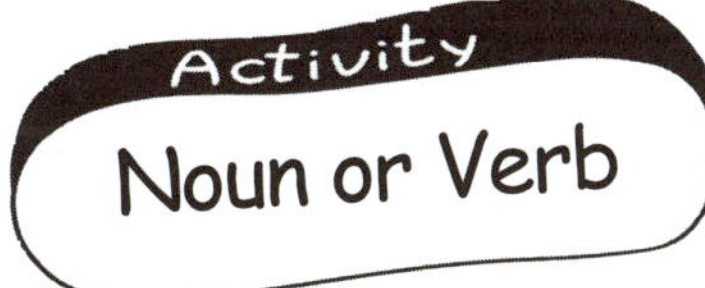

Activity
Noun or Verb

단어에는 여우(fox), 꼬리(tail)과 같이 이름을 나타내는 단어 ' 명사 ' 와
말하다(say), 앉다(sit)와 같이 동작을 나타내는 단어 ' 동사 ' 가 있답니다.
Word Box에 있는 단어들을 찾아 관련 있는 것끼리 모아보세요.

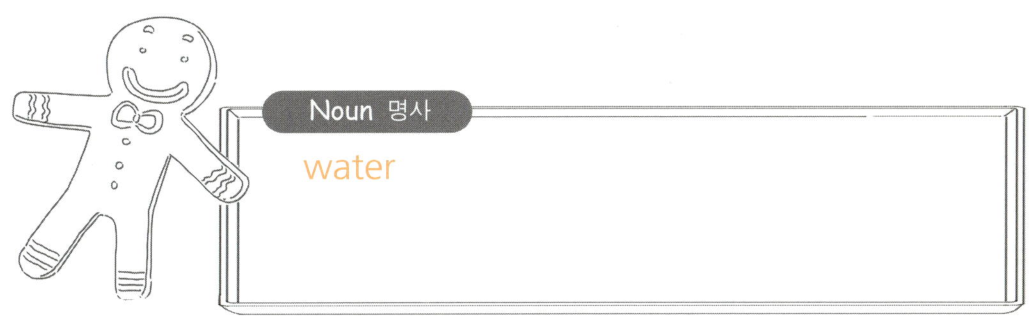

Noun 명사

water

Verb 동사

catch

Word Box	water	catch	cow	man	run	follow	pig	make
	mouth	eat	tease	fox	toss	back	reach	river

31

4

진저브레드 맨이 더 빨리 달렸습니다 / 그리고 소리쳤어요. //

"달려봐요, / 최대한 빨리 달려보시라고요. // 당신들은 날 잡지 못할걸요. //

난 진저브레드 맨이거든요." //

이제 / 젖소도 그를 뒤쫓아갔습니다 / 하지만 그는 너무 빨랐습니다. //

돼지가 진저브레드 맨을 보았습니다 / 그리고는 그를 쫓아갔습니다. //

"넌 날 군침 돌게 만드는구나. // 나는 널 먹고 싶어. // 멈춰!" //

5

노부부, 젖소, 그리고 돼지가 그를 쫓아갔습니다. //

진저브레드 맨이 웃었어요 / 그리고 그들을 놀려댔습니다. //

"너희들은 날 절대로 못 잡는다니까. // 내가 가장 빠르거든." //

그때 그는 강가에 다다랐습니다 / 그러자 그는 무서워졌죠. //

"아, 이런! // 내가 젖겠는걸. // 어떻게 이 강을 건너지?" //

여우가 지나가다가 말했어요, / "네가 강을 건너는 것을 내가 도와줄 수 있어." //

6

"내 꼬리 위에 앉아." / 여우가 그를 보면서 씨익 웃었습니다. //

여우는 헤엄치기 시작했습니다 / 그러자 곧 그는 젖게 되었습니다. //

"내 등 위로 올라오렴." / 여우가 말했습니다, / 그러자 그는 그렇게 했습니다. //

"넌 너무 무거워. // 내 코 위로 뛰어올라와." / 여우가 말했습니다. //

여우는 그를 공중 위로 가볍게 던져올렸습니다. / 그리고는 입을 벌렸습니다. //

"휙!" // 그게 바로 진저브레드 맨의 마지막이었습니다. //

Grammar Activity

Who is the fastest?
Who is the heaviest?

다음 그림을 잘 보고 알맞은 단어를 Word Box에서 찾아 문장을 완성하세요.

Word Box	fast faster fastest
	heavy heavier heaviest

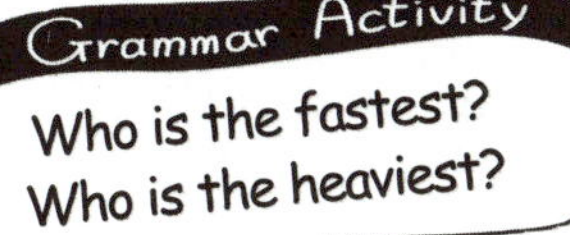

You are ___heavy___.

You are __________ than the gingerbread man.

You are the __________ of all.

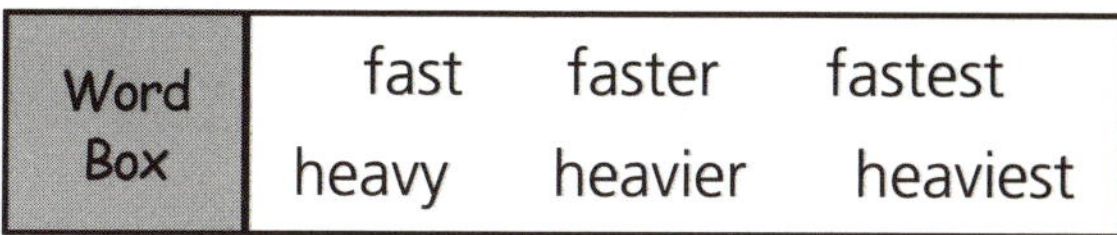

I am the __________ of all.

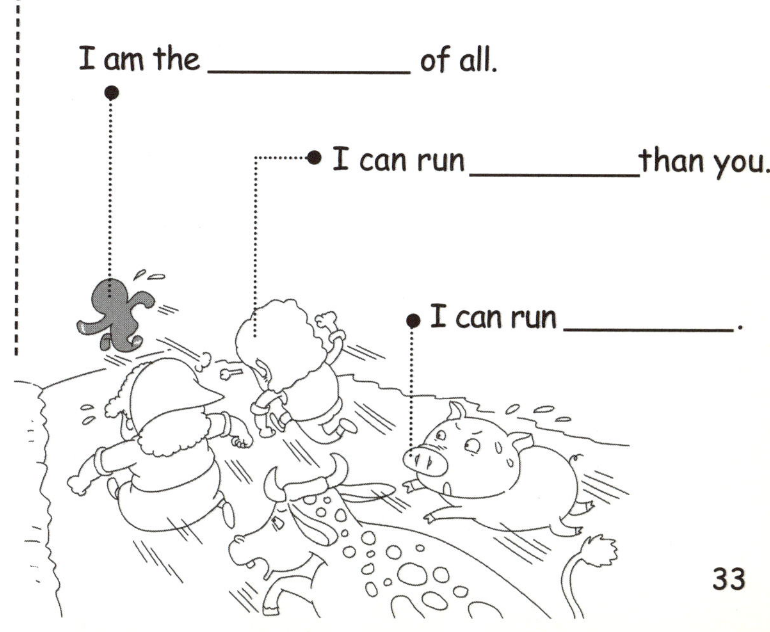

I can run __________ than you.

I can run __________.

Fill in the blanks. 빈 칸에 알맞은 단어를 고르세요.

1. _______________ was too fast, so nobody could catch him.

   a. The old man   b. The cow   c. The pig   d. The gingerbread man

2. The pig said, "You make my mouth water." It means that _______________.

   a. he is thirsty   b. he wants to brush his teeth

   c. he wants to eat the gingerbread man   d. he wants to drink water

3. The gingerbread man laughed and teased the old couple, the cow, and the pig

   because _______________________.

   a. they weren't fast   b. they were stupid

   c. they were wet   d. they were fast

4. The gingerbread man got scared when he reached a river because _______________.

   a. he didn't know what to do   b. he couldn't run fast

   c. he didn't know how to swim   d. he didn't want to get wet

5. Finally, _______________ ate the gingerbread man.

   a. the fox   b. the old man   c. the pig   d. the cow

True or False? 내용이 맞으면 T, 틀리면 F에 동그라미 하세요.

6. The pig made the old woman's mouth water.   T / F

7. The fox helped the gingerbread man cross the river safely.   T / F

8. The fox tossed the gingerbread man up in the air and ate him.   T / F

Draw a picture! 순서대로 그림을 그리고, 이름을 적어 보세요.

9. Who followed the gingerbread man?

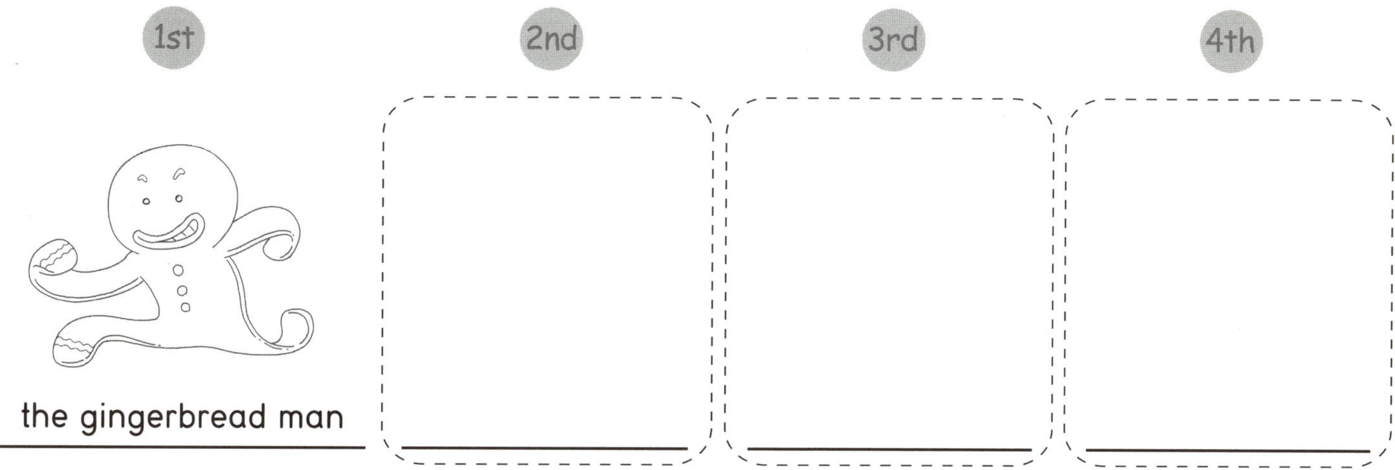

1st | 2nd | 3rd | 4th

the gingerbread man

Complete the story. Word Box 에 있는 단어를 이용하여 이야기의 줄거리를 완성해 보세요.

The old woman __________ a gingerbread man for __________________.
10 / 11

She put him in the oven, and then she __________ a little voice from it.
12

When she opened the oven, the gingerbread man jumped ____________ it.
13

The old couple _____________ him to __________ but he was too fast.
14 / 15

The ________ saw him and she ran ___________ the gingerbread man, too.
16 / 17

The pig ________ the gingerbread man and he wanted to eat him.
18

The pig also ran after him, but he was ________________.
19

The gingerbread man _______________ a river and he didn't want to get wet.
20

A fox tricked him and he ate the gingerbread man by himself.

Word Box
cow
saw
out of
made
heard
followed
catch
after
too fast
reached
Christmas

각 그림에 알맞은 대화문을 Sentence Box에서 찾아 만화를 완성하세요.

Sentence Box

a. Don't eat me!

b. I can't wait to eat it.

c. Come back!

d. It will be delicious!

1

*할머니: 근사해 보이는걸! 맛있을 거야!

*할아버지: 먹고 싶어서 못 참겠군. 냄새가 정말 좋은걸.

2

*진저브레드 맨: 절 먹지 말아요! 날 잡을 수 있으면 잡아봐요!

*할아버지: 맙소사! *할머니: 멈춰! 돌아오라고!

3

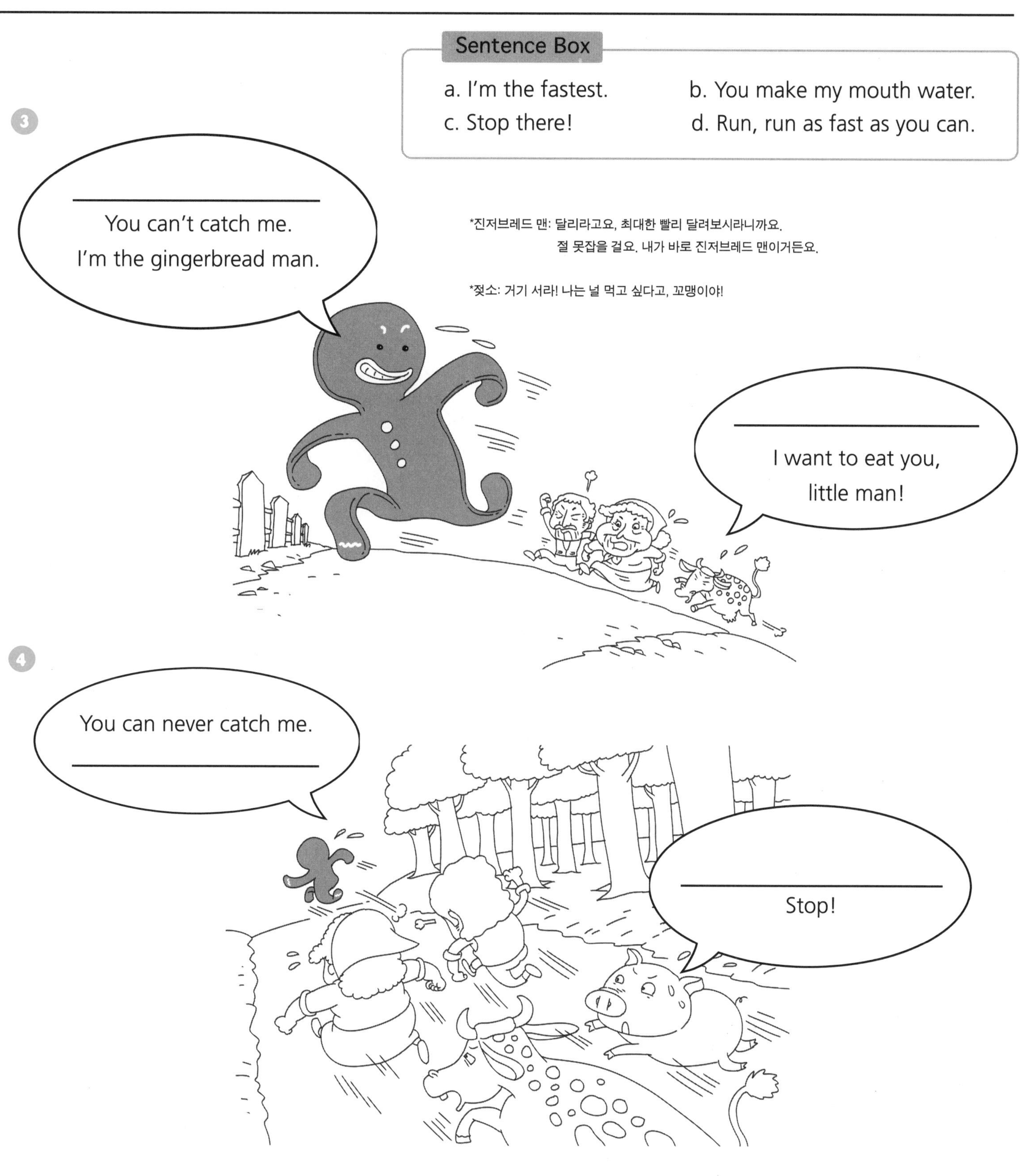

*진저브레드 맨: 달리라고요, 최대한 빨리 달려보시라니까요.
절 못잡을 걸요. 내가 바로 진저브레드 맨이거든요.

*젖소: 거기 서라! 나는 널 먹고 싶다고, 꼬맹이야!

4

*진저브레드 맨: 여러분은 절대로 날 못 잡는다니까요. 내가 제일 빠르거든요.
*돼지: 날 군침 돌게 만드는군. 나는 널 먹고 싶어. 멈춰!

Sentence Box

a. I can help you cross the river.
b. climb onto my back
c. I will get wet.
d. Sit on my tail.
e. You are too heavy.
f. How can I cross the river?

1

한 할아버지와 할머니가 오두막집에 살고 있었어요.

할머니가 크리스마스를 맞이해서 진저브레드 맨을 만들었습니다.

"눈에는 건포도를, 그리고 단추에는 체리를!

근사한 걸! 맛있을 거야." 할머니가 말했어요.

할머니는 그를 오븐 안으로 넣었습니다.

"먹고 싶어서 참을 수가 없군. 냄새가 정말 좋은걸." 할아버지가 말했어요.

2

그때 갑자기, 할머니는 오븐 안에서 작은 목소리를 들었습니다.

"문 좀 열어줘요! 당장 밖으로 나가고 싶다고요."

"너인 게냐?" 할머니가 조심스럽게 오븐을 열었습니다.

진저브레드 맨이 오븐 밖으로 뛰쳐나왔습니다.

그리고는 창문 밖으로 뛰어나갔습니다.

"절 먹지 마세요!" 진저브레드 맨이 외쳤습니다.

"멈춰! 돌아오라고!" 노부부가 소리지르며 그를 따라갔습니다.

진저브레드 맨은 말을 하면서 계속 달렸습니다.

"달리라고요, 최대한 빨리 달려보시라니까요. 여러분은 날 절대로 못 잡을 걸요.

내가 바로 진저브레드 맨이거든요."

젖소가 진저브레드 맨을 보고는 말했어요.

"거기 서지 못해! 내가 너를 먹고 싶다고, 꼬맹이야."

진저브레드 맨이 더 빨리 달리면서 소리쳤어요.

"달려보시죠. 최대한 빨리 달려보시라고요. 당신들은 날 잡지 못할걸요.

난 진저브레드 맨이거든요."

이제 젖소도 그를 뒤쫓아 갔지만, 그는 너무 빨랐습니다.

돼지가 진저브레드 맨을 보고는 그를 쫓아갔습니다.

"날 군침 돌게 만드는군. 나는 널 먹고 싶어. 멈춰!"

노부부, 젖소, 그리고 돼지가 그를 쫓아갔습니다.

진저브레드 맨이 웃으며 그들을 놀려댔습니다.

"너희들은 날 절대로 못 잡는다니까. 내가 제일 빠르거든."

그때 그는 강가에 다다랐고 무서워졌습니다.

"아, 이런! 젖겠는걸. 강을 어떻게 건너지?"

여우가 지나가다가 말했어요, "내가 강 건너는 것을 도와줄 수 있는데."

"내 꼬리 위에 앉아." 여우가 그를 보면서 씨익 웃었습니다.

여우는 헤엄치기 시작했고, 진저브레드 맨은 곧 젖게 되었습니다.

"내 등 위로 올라오렴." 여우가 말했고, 그는 그렇게 하였습니다.

"넌 너무 무거워. 내 코로 뛰어올라와." 여우가 말했습니다.

여우는 그를 공중 위로 던져올리고는 입을 벌렸습니다.

"휙!" 그게 바로 진저브레드 맨의 마지막이었습니다.

Crossword Puzzle

각 문장에 알맞은 단어를 찾아 퍼즐을 완성하세요. 그리고 색 칸 안에 있는 글자만을 모아 정답을 찾아보세요.

Across

1 ___Raisins___ for eyes and cherries for buttons.

2 The gingerbread man laughed and ___________ the old couple.

3 The fox began to swim and soon he got ___________.

4 The old couple, a cow, and a pig ___________ the gingerbread man.

5 "You make my mouth___________. I want to eat you."

6 Now the cow also ________ after him, too.

Down

5 "I can't ___________ to eat it. It smells so good," said the man.

7 He reached a river and he got ___________.

8 The pig ___________ the gingerbread man and ran after him.

9 Suddenly, the woman heard a little ___________ from the oven.

10 The gingerbread man ran ___________ and shouted.

ANSWER | a | | e | s | t |

₁₀ ₇ ₂

Word Search

✏️ 다음 단어들을 찾아서 동그라미 하세요. 단어들은 가로, 세로, 거꾸로 숨어 있습니다.

A S M G O A T F R A
D L R Q U C N P I G
H B L Y H L I O N Y
I C N I M C E B J H
U O Q F G T Q M J W
N W X Y E A J S A F
E B O R A W T J R C
V M F C G N M O D Q
O X D H L F B U R H
D U S L E O P A R D

Animals

- GOAT 염소
- ALLIGATOR 악어
- COW 젖소
- OX 황소
- CAMEL 낙타
- DOVE 비둘기
- EAGLE 독수리
- FOX 여우
- LEOPARD 표범
- LION 사자
- PIG 돼지

D S U G A R T S E G
E L R D V T N P G I
T B E A F L I E N N
A C T I I A E N J G
L J T F G S Y M K E
O K U Y L A I M C R
C F B R A O T N R T
O M A G V S U O D R
H S D C H E R R Y E
C U X P U R Y S W Z

Cookies

- EGG 달걀
- CHOCOLATE 초콜릿
- GINGER 생강
- CHERRY 체리
- RAISIN 건포도
- BUTTER 버터
- SALT 소금
- FLOUR 밀가루
- SUGAR 설탕
- SYRUP 시럽

The woman made a gingerbread man.
할머니는 진저브레드 맨을 만들었습니다.

He ran out the window.
그는 창문 밖으로 뛰어나갔습니다.

They yelled and followed him.
그들은 소리치며 그를 쫓아갔습니다.

The cow ran after him, too.
젖소도 그를 뒤쫓아갔습니다.

The fox grinned at him.
여우는 그를 보면서 씨익 웃었습니다.

The fox began to swim.
여우는 헤엄치기 시작했습니다.

He reached a river.
그는 강가에 다다랐습니다.

The fox tossed him up in the air.
여우는 그를 공중 위로 가볍게 던져올렸습니다.

Activity: What was it?

P.13
그림을 보고, 무엇인지 빈칸을 채워 보세요. 그리고 과거에는 어떤 모습이었는지 관련 있는 그림을 찾아 연결해 보세요.

1) 
Now it is a ______cottage______.
What was it?

2)
Now it is a _gingerbread man_.
What was it?

3)
Now it is a ______raisins______.
What was it?

Activity: Find Opposites

P.15
다음 단어들의 반대말을 쓰고, 번호를 이용하여 gingerbread man이 하는 말을 완성해 보세요.

do	↔	d o n ' t (9)
man	↔	w o m a n (10 8)
here	↔	t h e r e (4 6 7)
I	↔	Y o u (2)
close	↔	o p e n (1 5 3)

Activity: Spelling Errors

P.17
영어 철자(spelling)를 주의 깊게 보세요. 철자가 올바르게 쓰여 있는 공간만 예쁘게 색칠해 보세요.

Q. What can you find from this picture?

A. I can find a ______gingerbread______ ______girl______.

Grammar Activity: Complete the sentences!

P.19
알맞은 단어를 골라 문장을 완성하세요.

1. An old man and old woman (liveed, (lived), livd) in a cottage.

2. The woman (maked, makd, (made)) a gingerbread man for Christmas.

3. The old woman ((put), putted, puted) him in the oven.

4. The gingerbread man (runned, runed, (ran)) out the window.

5. The old man (sayed, (said), sayd) to the woman.

6. The cow (seed, (saw), see) the gingerbread man.

7. The old couple ((yelled), yellled, yellt) loudly.

8. Suddenly, the old woman (heared, (heard), herd) a little voice.

Activity — Unscramble words

결국 영리한 여우가 혼자 진저브레드를 먹게 됐네요. 여우가 무슨 말을 했는지, 아래 뒤섞여 있는 낱말들을 순서대로 다시 써 보면 알 수 있답니다. 회색으로 표시된 글자만을 모아 순서대로 쓰세요.

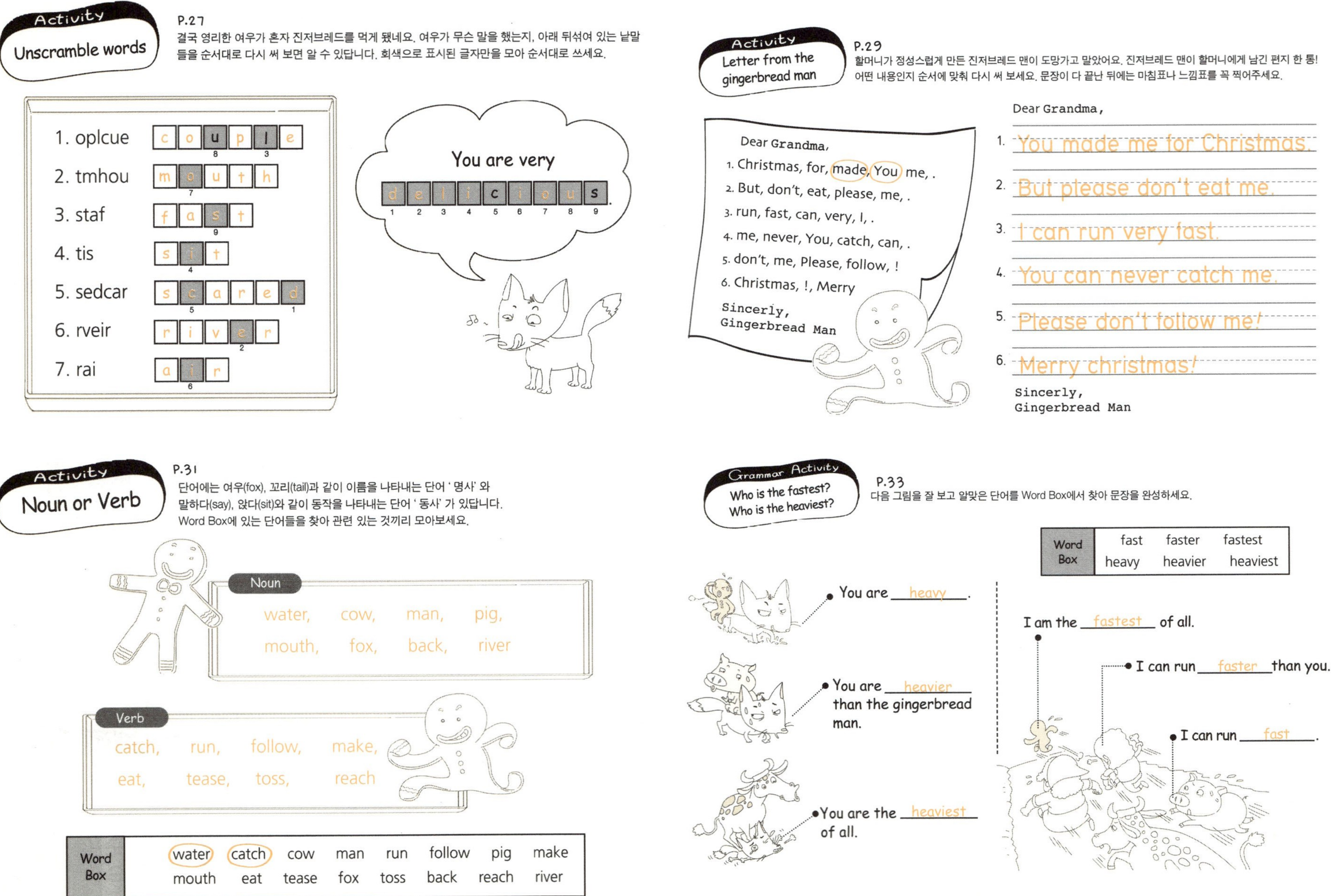

1. oplcue — c o u p l e
2. tmhou — m o u t h
3. staf — f a s t
4. tis — s i t
5. sedcar — s c a r e d
6. rveir — r i v e r
7. rai — a i r

Activity — Letter from the gingerbread man

P.29
할머니가 정성스럽게 만든 진저브레드 맨이 도망가고 말았어요. 진저브레드 맨이 할머니에게 남긴 편지 한 통! 어떤 내용인지 순서에 맞춰 다시 써 보세요. 문장이 다 끝난 뒤에는 마침표나 느낌표를 꼭 찍어주세요.

Dear Grandma,
1. You made me for Christmas.
2. But please don't eat me.
3. I can run very fast.
4. You can never catch me.
5. Please don't follow me!
6. Merry christmas!

Sincerly,
Gingerbread Man

Activity — Noun or Verb

P.31
단어에는 여우(fox), 꼬리(tail)과 같이 이름을 나타내는 단어 '명사' 와 말하다(say), 앉다(sit)와 같이 동작을 나타내는 단어 '동사' 가 있답니다. Word Box에 있는 단어들을 찾아 관련 있는 것끼리 모아보세요.

Noun
water, cow, man, pig, mouth, fox, back, river

Verb
catch, run, follow, make, eat, tease, toss, reach

Word Box	water	catch	cow	man	run	follow	pig	make
	mouth	eat	tease	fox	toss	back	reach	river

Grammar Activity — Who is the fastest? Who is the heaviest?

P.33
다음 그림을 잘 보고 알맞은 단어를 Word Box에서 찾아 문장을 완성하세요.

Word Box	fast	faster	fastest
	heavy	heavier	heaviest

- You are heavy.
- You are heavier than the gingerbread man.
- You are the heaviest of all.

I am the fastest of all.

I can run faster than you.

I can run fast.

1st week P.20~21

1. ⓑ The old woman made a <u>gingerbread man</u> for Christmas.

2. ⓒ The old woman used <u>raisins</u> for eyes and <u>cherries</u> for buttons.

3. ⓒ The gingerbread man could <u>run and talk</u>.

4. ⓐ <u>The man</u> couldn't wait to eat the gingerbread man because it smelled so good.

5. ⓒ <u>The old couple</u> yelled and followed <u>the gingerbread man</u>.

6. ⓓ <u>The old couple and the cow</u> wanted to eat the gingerbread man.

7. ⓐ The gingerbread man could run <u>fast</u>.

8. F   9. F

10. the old woman   11. the gingerbread man   12. the cow

13. <u>The woman heard a little voice from the oven.</u>

14. <u>The gingerbread man jumped out of the oven.</u>

15. <u>Run as fast as you can!</u>

2nd week P.34~35

1. ⓓ <u>The gingerbread man</u> was to fast, so nobody could catch him.

2. ⓒ The pig said, "You make my mouth water." It means that <u>he wants to eat the gingerbread man</u>.

3. ⓐ The gingerbread man laughed and teased the old couple, the cow, and the pig because <u>they weren't fast</u>.

4. ⓓ The gingerbread man got scared when he reached a river because <u>he didn't want to get wet</u>.

5. ⓐ Finally, <u>the fox</u> ate the gingerbread man.

6. F   7. F   8. T

9.  

<u>the old couple</u>   <u>the cow</u>   <u>the pig</u>

10. made   11. Christmas   12. heard

13. out of   14. followed   15. catch

16. cow   17. after   18. saw

19. too fast   20. reached

Crossword Puzzle

Word Search

Animals

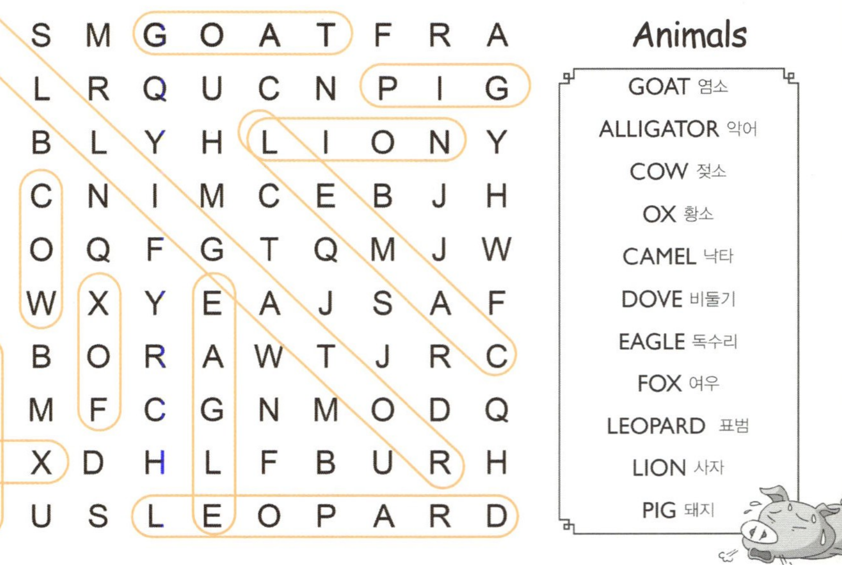

Cookies

-THE END-

WiSe kids

8

The Gingerbread Man

This book belongs to _____________

1

An old man and an old woman lived in a cottage.

The woman made a gingerbread man for Christmas.

"Raisins for eyes and cherries for buttons!

It looks great! It will be delicious," said the woman.

She put him in the oven.

"I can't wait to eat it. It smells so good,"

said the man.

"Sit on my tail," the fox grinned at him.

The fox began to swim and soon he got wet.

"Climb onto my back," said the fox and he did.

"You are too heavy. Jump on my nose," said the fox.

The fox tossed him up in the air

and opened her mouth.

"Snap!" That was the end of the gingerbread man.

The old couple, a cow, and a pig chased him.
The gingerbread man laughed and teased them.
"You can never catch me. I'm the fastest."
Then he reached a river and he got scared.
"Oh no! I will get wet. How can I cross the river?"
A fox came by and said,
"I can help you cross the river."

6

Suddenly, the woman heard a little voice
 from the oven.
"Open the door! I want to get out right now."
"Is that you?" She opened the oven carefully.
The gingerbread man jumped out of the oven.
Then he ran out the window.
"Don't eat me!" yelled the gingerbread man.

3

"Stop! Come back!" They yelled and followed him.
The gingerbread man ran on, saying,
"Run, run as fast as you can. You can't catch me.
I'm the gingerbread man."
The cow saw the gingerbread man and she said,
"Stop there! I want to eat you, little man."

The gingerbread man ran faster and shouted,
"Run, run as fast as you can. You can't catch me.
I'm the gingerbread man."
Now the cow ran after him too,
but he was too fast.
The pig saw the gingerbread man and ran after him.
"You make my mouth water. I want to eat you. Stop!"